Illustrators
Janet Blakeley/N E Middleton
Richard Hook/Temple Art (cover)
Elaine Lee/N E Middleton
Jim Robins/N E Middleton
Ken Stott/N E Middleton

First published in 1982 by Macdonald Educational
under the title
Peoples of the Past: Everyday Life in the Sixteenth Century

Reprinted in 1993
by Simon & Schuster Young Books
Campus 400
Maylands Avenue
Hemel Hempstead, Herts HP2 7EZ

Photographs
Aldus Archive 56(B)
Courtesy of the Trustees of the British Museum 14, 16
Giraudon 12(T)
Hever Castle 18
J. Allan Cash 29, 31(B)
Kunsthistorisches Museum, Vienna 23, 39, 41
The Mansell Collection 31(T), 32, 57(B)
Mary Evans Picture Library 28
MAS/El Escorial 44
MAS/Museo del Prado 17
Musee des Beaux Arts, Lausanne
Museum Boymans van Beuningen, Rotterdam 35
National Scheepvart Museum, Antwerp 52–3
Narodni Gallery, Prague 33
Reproduced by Gracious Permission of her Majesty
    The Queen 8–9
Robert Harding Picture Library 21(R)
Scala/Bibliotheca Nationale, Firenze 56(T)

Scala/Palazzo Vecchio, Firenze 57(T)
Ullstein Bilderdienst 37
Victoria and Albert Museum 55
Woodmansterne Ltd. 27
Zefa 12(B), 21(L), 30

ISBN 0-7500-1468-7

A catalogue record for this book is available from the
    British Library.

Printed and bound in Belgium by Proost International
    Book Production

Everyday Life in
Tudor Times

Haydn Middleton

SIMON & SCHUSTER
YOUNG BOOKS

Contents

Introduction

Four hundred years ago Europe was very different from what it is today. England and Scotland each had its own royal family. There were no countries called Italy and Germany. The Netherlands belonged to the King of Spain, who was the most powerful Christian monarch. And, from the East, the Turks were threatening the whole continent.

The everyday lives of European people were very different, too. Half the babies born died before their first birthdays. Anyone of forty was thought very old. There were many plagues and diseases, and doctors could do little to cure them.

Women were strictly controlled by their fathers or husbands. They existed only to serve men, who were thought to be the masters. However, for much of this period England was ruled by a queen, Elizabeth I.

The rich and the poor lived completely different lives. The rich ate fantastic meals, wore gorgeous clothes and lived in beautiful homes. They paid few taxes, and made sure their children had a good education.

But there were far more poor people than rich people. The poor often went hungry. They wore simple, home-made clothes and rarely changed them. The homes of the poorest were tumbledown shacks, which they shared with their animals. They had very little money, but had to pay many taxes. Most poor people could not read or write, and their children did not go to school or university.

Life was very hard for most people. But they still found ways to enjoy themselves, and felt sure that God was watching over them. Life on Earth was not so important, getting to Heaven was what really mattered.

Rulers of Europe

In the 16th century kings and queens lived in spectacular style. As they paraded from one magnificent palace to another, they struck awe and respect into their subjects. The power of royal families, like the Tudors in England, was immense. Parliaments played little part in the running of kingdoms and empires.

It was important for rulers to provide law and order, so their subjects could go about their business in safety. This meant ruthlessly crushing any rebellions. The usual price of disobedience was death. King Henry VIII of England executed a close friend, Sir Thomas More, who did not obey him.

Although most rulers were men, the English queen, Elizabeth I, was one of the most highly-respected rulers of the time. Problems arose when a child came to the throne. During the reign of the French boy-king Charles IX, a group of nobles seized power. Since the king could not keep the peace, France was almost destroyed by feuding.

▼ In June 1520, Henry VIII of England met Francis I of France at the Field of the Cloth of Gold, near Calais. Enormously expensive feasts and entertainments were laid on for the kings and their men. This painting shows the arrival of King Henry (bottom left).

Henry and Francis did not stay friends for long. Two years later they were at war with one another.

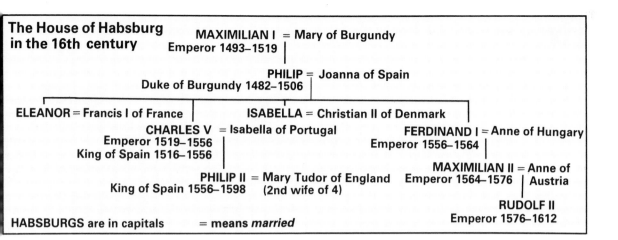

The House of Habsburg in the 16th century

MAXIMILIAN I = Mary of Burgundy
Emperor 1493–1519

PHILIP = Joanna of Spain
Duke of Burgundy 1482–1506

ELEANOR = Francis I of France

ISABELLA = Christian II of Denmark

CHARLES V = Isabella of Portugal
Emperor 1519–1556
King of Spain 1516–1556

FERDINAND I = Anne of Hungary
Emperor 1556–1564

PHILIP II = Mary Tudor of England
King of Spain 1556–1598   (2nd wife of 4)

MAXIMILIAN II = Anne of
Emperor 1564–1576 | Austria

RUDOLF II
Emperor 1576–1612

HABSBURGS are in capitals   = means *married*

Most rulers tried to add to their lands by warfare and marriage. The Habsburg family of Austria built up the greatest empire in Europe. From 1519 to 1555, Emperor Charles V ruled territories stretching from Spain to Hungary, and from Italy to the Netherlands.

▲ *The Habsburgs usually married into other ruling families. They enlarged their empire like this.*

▼ *This map shows western Europe in 1550. The Habsburgs seemed to be everywhere. A Habsburg was usually elected to rule over the Holy Roman Empire too.*

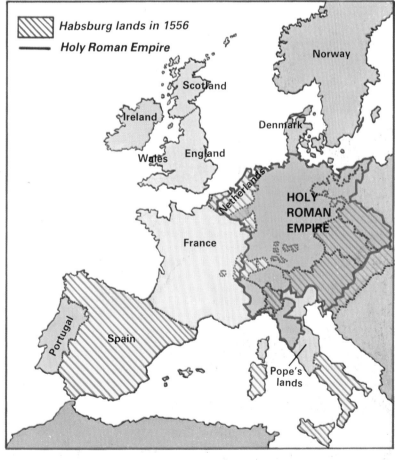

Habsburg lands in 1556

Holy Roman Empire

Norway

Scotland

Ireland

Denmark

Wales   England

Netherlands

HOLY
ROMAN
EMPIRE

France

Portugal

Spain

Pope's
lands

Europe and the world

Until the last years of the 15th century, Europeans knew very little about the rest of the world. They had made contact with distant empires in the East, but they had no idea that America existed. By 1600, all this had changed. Curiosity did not cause this 'Age of Discovery'; trade and religion did.

The sailors of Portugal and Spain were the first to brave the oceans. In 1498 the Portuguese sailed around the southern tip of Africa and reached India. They went on to trade with India, the Spice Islands (the East Indies), China and Japan. The inhabitants of most of these places looked down on the Portuguese. Few of them wanted to copy European customs or become Christian.

The Spaniards tried to get to Asia by sailing westwards. When they reached America they believed that it was Asia. But, as they explored the new lands, they realized that they had discovered a 'New World', rich in gold and silver.

The Spaniards brutally crushed the civilizations of Mexico and Peru. Then they set up their own vast American

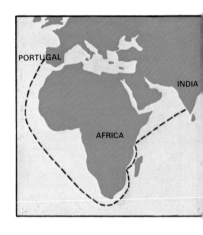

▲ The route of the first sea expedition from Europe to India, led by Vasco da Gama. He left Portugal in mid-1497, and arrived in India almost a year later.

▶ A Spanish captain telling the Incas of Peru to become Christians or be killed.
The Incas had never seen horses before the Spaniards arrived in 1531. They thought these strange beings might be gods. But the Spaniards behaved more like devils when they destroyed the Inca Empire.

► This is a scene in 16th-century Goa, from a book by an explorer about his travels. Goa was a large seaport in western India. In 1510, the Portuguese captured it and made it their chief port in Asia. From here, valuable spices like pepper, cinnamon and cloves were shipped back to Europe.

▼ In 1580 Queen Elizabeth I of England knighted Francis Drake on board his ship, the 'Golden Hind'. He had just returned from a three-year expedition round the world. Elizabeth called Drake her 'little master thief', because he brought back a massive haul of treasure taken from Spanish ships.

empire. At the same time, the Portuguese followed the Spaniards across the Atlantic, founding a huge colony in Brazil.

In 1580, King Philip II of Spain seized the Portuguese crown and empire. This made him the first ruler with territories stretching round the world.

Religion and the people

In the 16th century men and women worried about life after death. They relied on the Church to tell them how to live good lives on Earth, and hoped that God would reward them when they died. At the start of the century, all the countries of western Europe were Catholic.

The Church was far more important than it is today. Church-bells announced the time for work or meals or rest. Church law-courts enforced Christian behaviour. Monasteries acted as schools, inns and hospitals. Bishops and cardinals were among a monarch's most trusted advisers.

The Church had become immensely rich. Many clergymen cared more for wealth and pleasure than for their religious duties. Critics protested about the state of the Church, and suggested ways to improve it. The authorities took little notice. So these 'Protestants' began setting up their own churches.

By the middle of the century, western Europe was split between Protestants and Roman Catholics. Both believed theirs was the true form of Christianity – and were prepared to fight to prove it. So Europe was torn apart by a series of savage wars, fought in God's name.

▲ Martin Luther, a German professor, started to complain about the Church in 1517. Eventually, he set up his own 'Protestant' or 'Lutheran' church.

◄ The Escorial, a 16th-century monastery and palace outside Madrid. It was built for the Catholic King Philip II of Spain.

On the eve of St Bartholomew's Day, 1572, Catholics in France turned on the Protestants and slaughtered them. This painting shows the horrifying scenes in Paris. In the centre, the Catholic King Charles IX is inspecting the cut-off head of a Protestant leader.

► By 1550, Europe was a patchwork of different religions. Most people followed the religion of their rulers, to avoid being persecuted for their faith.

▼ A family studying the Bible. People often worshipped at home and in church. Richer families employed their own chaplains.

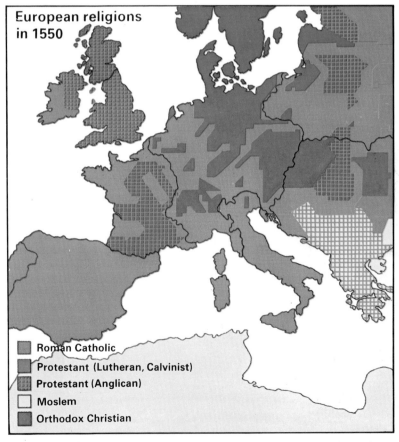

European religions in 1550

- ▨ Roman Catholic
- ▨ Protestant (Lutheran, Calvinist)
- ▦ Protestant (Anglican)
- ☐ Moslem
- ▨ Orthodox Christian

The Great Chain

The rulers of Europe needed endless supplies of money. It was expensive to fight wars and build palaces. Royal servants had to be paid to run the government. An enormous increase in prices all over Europe made matters worse.

One way to raise more money was to demand higher taxes from the people. In many parts of Europe, rich nobles and Church officials did not have to pay these taxes. Instead, the peasants who were already suffering terribly from the rise in prices had to pay. The peasants paid taxes to their ruler, to their local lord and to their local clergy.

Today we believe that all people should be treated the same. But people in the 16th century believed that they were part of a 'Great Chain', created by God. This Chain stretched from God down to lifeless objects. Everyone and everything had a place in the Chain. People stood higher than animals, plants and stones. But clergymen and nobles stood higher than gentlemen and peasants, and above them all stood kings.

If you accepted your place on Earth, you were doing God's will, and would be rewarded in Heaven. But if you rebelled against your 'superiors', you were disobeying God, and could expect dreadful punishments after death.

▲ *This German picture from 1532 shows the Chain in the form of a tree. There are peasants at the top as well as at the bottom!*

▼ *In England, ordinary folk were controlled by men like these.*

Bishop's steward

Churchwarden

Lord of the manor

Justice of the Peace

Taille (tax on people)

Seigneurial dues

◀ *Even if a French peasant farmer had a good harvest, the crops and any money he got from selling them was not all his own. He had to pay many taxes, dues to his local lord, and one-tenth of his income (a tithe) went to the Church.*

Gabelle (tax on salt)

Tithe

Therefore, most people near the bottom of the Chain put up with misery on Earth to avoid the torments of Hell. So there were few protests against the heavy taxes.

▼ *In 1525 a penny (½p) bought 10 eggs, 3.5 litres of milk, 6 herrings, a chicken and 4 small loaves of bread.*

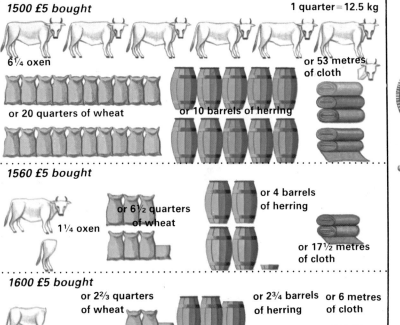

1500 £5 bought

1 quarter = 12.5 kg

6¼ oxen

or 20 quarters of wheat

or 10 barrels of herring

or 53 metres of cloth

1560 £5 bought

1¼ oxen

or 6½ quarters of wheat

or 4 barrels of herring

or 17½ metres of cloth

1600 £5 bought

or 2⅔ quarters of wheat

or 2¾ barrels of herring

or 6 metres of cloth

¾ ox

▼ *In 1525 a groat (2p) bought half a kilo of beef, a kilo of mutton, a pair of shoes, a kilo of candles, 1.5 litres of wine and a kilo of soap.*

◀ *Prices rose very fast in the 16th century. The chart shows the difference between what £5 (a very large sum in those days) bought in 1500, in 1560 and in 1600.*

15

Health and hygiene

Everyone, whatever their position in the 'Great Chain', lived surrounded by disease and death. Influenza, smallpox and bubonic plague swept across Europe. The worst effects were felt in towns and cities, where large numbers of people were crowded together in filthy conditions. In 1599, for example, 4000 of the 4500 inhabitants of Santander in Spain died of the plague.

Doctors could not explain these diseases, let alone cure them. When Milan was hit by plague in 1576, 'servants of the devil' were blamed. They were supposed to have dropped poison into the holy water in the churches. Doctors and surgeons could only deal with less mysterious ailments. Those who could not afford to pay doctors' fees used herbs as cures.

By modern standards, 16th-century people were hopelessly unhygienic. Soap was very expensive, and people rarely washed. Even kings like Henry IV of France used special perfumes to drown their dreadful body odours. So imagine what their subjects smelled like!

▲ Wash-day for some German peasant women. The cloth is boiled, beaten and rinsed, then hung out to dry, or laid out in the sun to bleach.

▼ Barber-shops were sometimes surgeries too. Here, one barber-surgeon has pulled out a bad tooth, while another is sawing off part of a poisoned leg. Patients had to go through operations without painkillers. The customer on the right is having lice removed from his scalp.

▲ The Flemish artist Pieter Bruegel (died 1569) painted this extraordinary picture in 1562. It is called The Triumph of Death, and is meant to show how violent and dangerous life could be. The skeletons are the army of the dead, who have come back to Earth to carry off the living.

Surgical instruments

▲ An extractor, used for pulling out teeth.

▲ A saw, used for cutting off diseased limbs.

▲ Forceps, used during operations.

▲ A surgical drill, operated by hand.

◄ Few barber-surgeons had proper qualifications for their work. They relied on a steady hand! Their medical instruments were extremely primitive. No-one understood how important it was to keep them or the 'surgery' clean.

Clothes

Clothes in the 16th century were not just a matter of personal taste. Rulers like Queen Elizabeth I of England and King Philip II of Spain used their magnificent clothes to show their subjects just how rich and powerful they were. Most of those subjects wore simple woollen clothes, which were usually home-made.

Few people could afford to dress fashionably. For most of the period, wealthy men and women copied the styles worn at the Spanish court. Then, towards the end of the century, they began to look to France for new ideas. There were no fashion magazines, but by 1600, small dolls dressed in the latest styles were being sent from Paris to those who wanted to, and could afford to, keep in touch with the trends.

People's clothes also showed their position in the 'Great

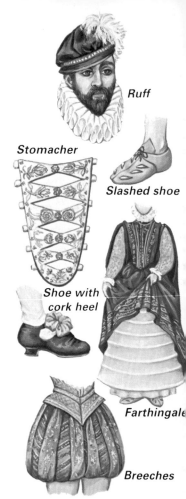

Ruff

Stomacher

Slashed shoe

Shoe with cork heel

Farthingale

Breeches

◀ Queen Elizabeth I, like all fashionable ladies, made great use of cosmetics. Bright red lips on a snow-white face were thought to be very beautiful.

French gentleman

◄ Fashionable clothes were expensive and impractical. Elegant, but flimsy, shoes were made of velvet, silk or soft leather. Women's stomachers and men's breeches were covered with lavish embroidery. Sometimes they were slashed, to show off different material underneath. Women wore frames called 'farthingales' under their gowns, to make the skirts stand out.

Chain'. The rulers of Europe tried to keep their subjects in their proper places by passing laws saying who could wear what. In Paris during the reign of Henry IV, for example, only noblewomen could wear silk. But it was difficult to make people obey these laws. 'There is now such a mingle-mangle of apparel [dress],' an Englishman complained in 1585, 'that it is very hard to know who is a gentleman and who is not.'

▲ German peasants outside an inn. They are wearing simple, practical outfits in cheap materials. Hats were very popular.

▼ Richer people like these dressed to catch the eye. Poorer people could not afford silks, satins, velvets and furs.

Italian couple

Dutch merchant's wife

English lady with her children

Houses and homes

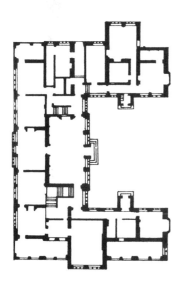

▲ *This is a bird's-eye view of Aston Hall, in Warwickshire. Great houses were often built in the shape of the letter 'E'.*

In the Middle Ages noblemen built their houses for protection. Inside the thick stone walls masters and servants lived together. At the end of the 15th century things started to change. The new cannons could break down the thickest walls. So the nobles decided that if their homes could not be safe, they could at least be comfortable. Starting in Italy, a craze for home-improvement and new building spread across Europe.

The Italians and the French were the first to divide up their big houses to make smaller rooms. Ceilings were put in, to make two floors where there had been only one. Upstairs, bedrooms were made. Parlours and kitchens were separated from other rooms. The French habit of putting the servants' quarters in the basements of town houses soon caught on in London.

Glass was now cheaper so houses had more and larger windows. Hardwick Hall, in England, was said to have 'more glass than wall', it had so many windows. Many

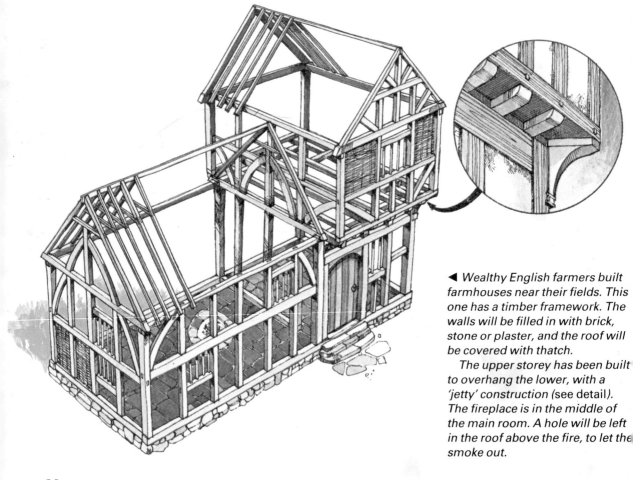

◄ *Wealthy English farmers built farmhouses near their fields. This one has a timber framework. The walls will be filled in with brick, stone or plaster, and the roof will be covered with thatch.*

The upper storey has been built to overhang the lower, with a 'jetty' construction (see detail). The fireplace is in the middle of the main room. A hole will be left in the roof above the fire, to let the smoke out.

◄ These peasants have a bare but quite comfortable home, with a separate room for their animals.

The windows are covered with linen, soaked in oil to make it transparent. Glass was still too expensive for poorer people.

houses were also fitted with ornamental chimneys, to take away smoke from the fireplace.

But very few people benefited from these improvements. In large cities like London, Naples and Madrid, the new houses of the rich stood next to the squalid, overcrowded dwellings of the poor. While the wealthy were building separate rooms for their servants, many peasants still slept and ate alongside their pigs and cattle.

▲ Some 16th-century merchants' houses are still standing in Amsterdam, in the Netherlands. They are packed together, and are very close to water. This was convenient, since journeys by water were usually quicker and safer than journeys by land.

◄ This is the beautiful château at Chenonceaux, in the valley of the river Loire in France. A château is a great country mansion, or even a small castle. This one was begun in 1515. In the past, water had been used for defensive moats. In the 16th century, it was used more often for decoration.

Furniture and furnishings

The poor could afford only the bare necessities of life. Furniture was a luxury. When someone died, an 'inventory' or list of their possessions was made. Surviving inventories show how little furniture the poor owned – often only a table, a bench and a few sacks of straw to sleep on.

The homes of people further up the 'Great Chain' were different. The large glass windows made rooms lighter, so wealthy people wanted furniture that was both beautiful and useful.

The parlour was usually the finest room. It might have carved wooden panelling on the walls, plaster patterns on the ceiling, and even colourful coats-of-arms in the windows. Carpets and tapestries were draped over wooden tables and chests. Rushes were scattered on the floor in winter, and herbs and flowers in the summer. If

▲ *Bedwarmers like these could be put under the bedclothes. The top one is a pan, which was filled with hot coals. The other one is a candle in a wooden cage.*

▼ *This four-poster bed is made of solid oak, and probably has a feather mattress. Two curtains pull right round the bed, to keep out draughts. The master's oak chair has arms, which were gradually coming into fashion.*

► Most rulers liked to surround themselves with beautiful furnishings and ornaments. The Italian craftsman Benvenuto Cellini made this salt-cellar and gave it to Francis I of France in 1543.

▼ People used cut-away beer-barrels for tables and chairs. They were especially common in Dutch inns.

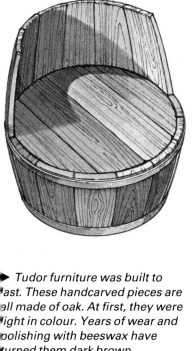

these were not changed regularly they became dirty and smelly.

By today's standards, houses were rather uncomfortable. Chairs with arms or padding were rare. There were no indoor toilets or bathrooms. Even the most luxurious houses were cold and smelt unpleasant.

► Tudor furniture was built to last. These handcarved pieces are all made of oak. At first, they were light in colour. Years of wear and polishing with beeswax have turned them dark brown.

23

Food and drink

The diet of most peasants was poor and boring. In an age of soaring prices, they could afford little more than bread. Sometimes they stirred the bread into watery vegetable stews. Meat was much too expensive for them. Fruit was quite common in southern Europe, although doctors believed it caused fevers. Since people depended on bread, a bad harvest could cause famine. In France alone there were thirteen major famines in the 16th century. At such times people ate almost anything – straw, roots, rats, even tree-bark!

By contrast, the rich ate an enormous variety of meat and fish. Meat was dried and salted to keep it through the winter. Then it was cooked in hot spices – to cover up the taste and smell of decay. Most vegetables were despised by the rich, although cabbages were thought to prevent baldness.

New delicacies, like turkeys and drinking chocolate from Mexico, provided variety now and then. Sugar was still an expensive luxury.

The people of southern Europe drank enormous amounts of wine. In the middle of the 16th century, each

▲ Carriers like this man sold water to many homes. The water was used more often for cooking than for washing.

▼ Special rooms were now set aside for eating. People ate with their hands, from pewter plates. Poorer families used wooden plates.

citizen of Valladolid in Spain consumed around a hundred litres a year. In northern Europe, home-brewed beer and sometimes cider were drunk by both adults and children. Water was often dirty, so drinking wine or beer was safer.

▲ Spanish nobles, or 'grandees', ate extremely well. They had delicacies imported from both Europe and America.

Their guests brought their own knives. They needed them to cope with the many meat dishes. In the year 1600 alone, 50,000 sheep, 12,000 oxen, 60,000 kids, 10,000 calves and 13,000 pigs were eaten in Madrid.

25

Family life

In the 16th century anyone over forty years of age was thought to be old. Children made up about half the population in most countries, even though half the babies born died before they were a year old. Those who survived were often killed by famine, disease or war before they were adults. In spite of this, the population was growing fast. In fact, some people feared that Europe was getting overcrowded. They need not have worried. The population of the British Isles is at least ten times bigger now than in 1600!

The father as head of the household was expected to rule his family as a king ruled his subjects. This meant that he often arranged marriages for his children.

Poor people usually got married later than rich people. They also had fewer children. A 16th-century proverb said 'Little wealth and many children bring great distress to many a man.'

Men controlled their wives almost as closely as their children. Compared to southern Europe, England was called 'a paradise for married women.' But even here, the

▲ This old man has made a contract with his children. He has agreed to give them his property, as long as they care for him until he dies. This was quite a common practice.

◄ Babies were christened very soon after they were born. This was because so many babies died, and their parents wanted to feel sure that their souls would go straight to heaven. There were no birth certificates in the 16th century, so many adults were not sure exactly how old they were.

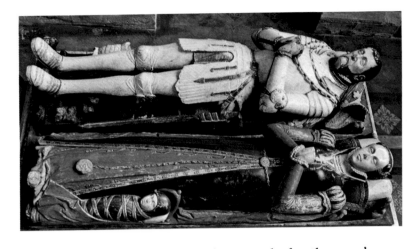

► *This beautifully coloured tomb is in Hereford Cathedral. The figures on top are models of the three people who are buried inside. The man is Alexander Denton, a gentleman who died in 1576 at the age of 31. The woman is his second wife, Anne, who died in 1566, when she was only 17. She died while giving birth to their child, who is also buried in the tomb. Only a wealthy family could have afforded an expensive tomb like this.*

Church taught that a woman 'was made for the man's use and benefit' – which usually meant a lifetime of domestic chores and child-bearing.

▼ *Once they were married, women were often expected to have a baby each year. They also had to run their households. Better-off women might have a nurse to look after their babies, and servants to help in the house, but there was still a great deal to do. These are just some of a woman's household jobs. Wool was carded to remove tangles before it was spun into thread.*

Preserving fish and meat for the winter

Baking bread

Shopping

Carding (right) and spinning wool

Cooking and mending

Going to school

Most boys had no education. They did not need to read or write, because their work depended on practical training and skill. Women's work was at home with the family, so girls, too, rarely had any education.

It was different for the sons of noblemen and the newer middle class, there were many schools for them. At the beginning of the century, most schools were part of churches or monasteries. They taught almost nothing but Latin grammar. This is where the term 'grammar school' came from. Boys who went to these schools went on to university or became priests.

There were few books, so long passages had to be learned by heart. Lessons could go on for ten hours a day, six days a week. The boys had to speak Latin, as well as to write it, and could be punished for speaking their own language. Even small offences were severely punished, usually with a beating.

Later in the century noblemen and merchants started schools in towns all over Europe. Very slowly teaching

▼ *Schoolmasters had no special training for their work. They were often priests. They were also very strict. A beating with the birch was a common punishment.*

◀ *This is Saint Ignatius Loyola (1491–1556). He set up many Jesuit schools in the Catholic parts of Europe. He was so interested in teaching and children, that he was made the patron saint of women who were expecting babies.*

▶ *Children often began their education with a 'horn-book' like this. Inside the wooden frame was a single page, which was protected by a thin, clear sheet of horn.*

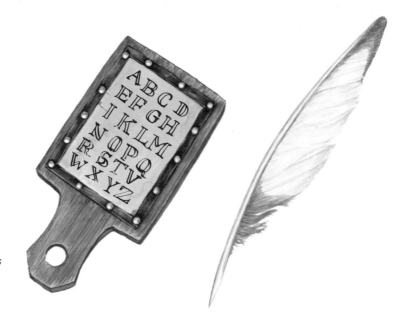

▲ *A bird's-feather quill pen for writing. Children usually sharpened their own quills with knives. They were also expected to mix their own ink.*

▼ *The Royal Grammar School in Guildford, Surrey, is still standing today, although it was built in Tudor times. Many other English schools are named after King Edward VI, the son of Henry VIII.*

became less rigid. Pupils were encouraged to find things out for themselves. Gradually acting, speechmaking, and even dancing and sport were included in school timetables. But Latin was still the most important subject.

Universities

In 16th-century England, there were only two universities – Oxford and Cambridge. They were founded to educate poor men's sons, who usually went on to become priests. But all over Europe, the sons of the wealthy were gradually squeezing out the poorer students.

A year or two at college had become a useful stepping-stone towards a career as a lawyer or a doctor, a businessman or a politician. Few of these richer undergraduates studied for long enough to gain a degree. Most of them went to university when they were about fourteen years old, and often preferred having a good time to working.

Students were watched over by tutors. A tutor taught his students, looked after them when they were ill, handed out their pocket money, and beat them if they misbehaved. In return for his services, he was paid by their fathers. Poor men simply could not afford to send their sons to university.

Serious students completed the full degree course after seven years. They studied subjects ranging from astronomy and the theory of music to theology. Students were tested in written examinations and also in 'disputations'. These were debates, in Latin, on a set topic between a student and his masters.

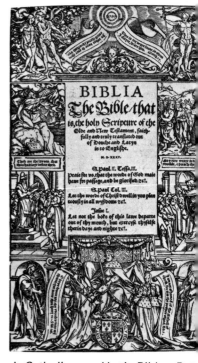

▲ Catholics used Latin Bibles. But the Protestants believed that this was wrong, because very few ordinary people could understand Latin. A scholar called Miles Coverdale was the first man to translate the whole Bible into English, and to have it printed. This is the title-page of his English Bible of 1535.

◀ The University of Salamanca, in Spain, was one of the greatest in 16th-century Europe. It had started as a cathedral school in the 13th century.

► Henry VIII's chief minister, Cardinal Thomas Wolsey, paid for this Oxford college to be built. He called it Cardinal College, after himself, but Henry later re-named it King's College. Eventually it was given its present name, Christ Church. The bell in the tower is still called 'Great Tom', after the Cardinal.

◄ This Oxford student is nearing the end of his seven-year course, when he will qualify as a Master of Arts. Many students had to pay for their own board and lodging. Poorer students raised money by doing odd jobs around the college, or by begging.

Work in the fields

In Europe in 1600, only about one person in every ten lived in a town. But the country people had to provide food and clothing for the townspeople, as well as for themselves.

The farm worker's day often began at dawn, and ended when it was too dark to see. Bread crops (wheat, barley, rye and oats), meat and milk were produced all over Europe. Other types of food varied from region to region. Cheese and bacon were common in the north. Oil, wine, fruit and beans were often produced in the south. Wool and hides, which could be made into clothing, came from livestock everywhere.

Some new crops were beginning to appear in Europe. Maize was imported from America, and grown in northern Italy. The potato had also been introduced from the New World. But farming methods were almost unchanged. Few people owned a plough, and fewer still owned a team of

▶ The owner of these fields separated his grazing land from his crop land. He 'enclosed' the fields with hedges. Sheep-farming had become very profitable, and farmers needed more pasture for their extra flocks. Sometimes they enclosed 'common land', which had once been used by poor peasants for their animals as well.

▼ The women on the left are picking vegetables called artichokes.
   The masked beekeeper (centre) had no trouble selling his honey. It was used to sweeten food before sugar became common.
   The men on the right are harvesting hops, which are used to make beer.

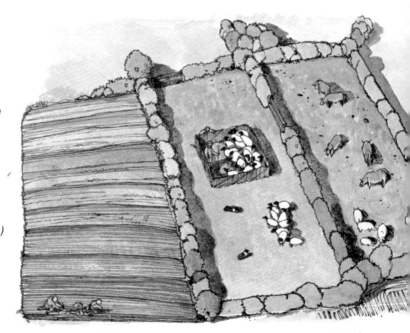

This woodcut shows activities in a farm in spring. In the background the soil is being harrowed to break it up, and in front a man is sowing seed by scattering it as he walks along the furrows.

cattle to pull the plough, and to supply manure to enrich the soil. Bread crops could not be grown on the same land for two years running. The soil had to be left to get back its richness, so fields lay unused for a year or more.

▲ *Ploughs were made of wood, and were often operated by hand. In the middle picture opposite, two men are furrowing the soil with one. But many poor peasant farmers could not afford even such simple tools.*

▼ *At hay-making everyone helped to get the hay in before rain spoilt it. Hay was very important as feed for livestock during the winter. Most people in Europe were involved in farmwork.*

Vagabonds and bandits

Vagabonds were people who either could not or would not work. They took to the roads and begged or stole. Many drifted into the larger towns, which were already over-crowded. Others joined any army that paid them for fighting.

The population was increasing so fast that there was a lot of competition for jobs. Most vagabonds just wandered around the country until they found work. But some people actually chose to beg and steal. Anyone caught begging was punished harshly. In England, a vagabond could be branded on the cheek with a 'V', and sent back to the place where he was born.

In southern Europe, the problem was more serious. In times of famine, hungry peasants flocked to join bandit gangs in the mountains and forests. They lived by robbing people. Governments tried to control them by using violence themselves. The heads of dead bandits were often stuck on spikes near a town's gates.

▼ Some beggars were wounded ex-soldiers. Others just pretended to be crippled, to win sympathy. Large towns attracted both beggars and those who really wanted to work. To try to solve the problem, local authorities in large English towns made attempts to help the poor.

► Travelling pedlars tramped the roads of Europe, selling cheap goods. This painting is by the Flemish artist Hieronymus Bosch, who died early in the 16th century. The pedlar, in his odd shoes, looks terribly shabby. The house in the background needs repairing. Paintings like this remind us how poor many people were.

▼ The roads of Europe were plagued by bandit gangs. These robbers were sometimes in league with innkeepers, who provided rooms for travellers. There were no police forces to fight crime but any bandits who were caught received little mercy.

Crime and punishment

Punishments in the 16th century seem terribly harsh today. In England, you could be slowly strangled to death for stealing goods worth more than one shilling. In parts of Italy, you could have your tongue ripped out for using the Lord's name as a swear-word. But many criminals were never caught. There were no police to track them down. So when a criminal was caught, he was severely punished, to make it clear to other people that crime did not pay. That is why executions were held in public.

Violence was more widespread than it is today. In the larger towns and cities, most people went about armed, to defend themselves against sudden attacks or robberies. Torture was the usual way of getting information out of criminals, then they were often hung, burned or boiled to death.

But criminals who had committed offences like stealing were often spared the harsh punishments laid down by law. In England, juries sometimes allowed thieves to go free instead of demanding the death penalty. They thought the punishment too severe.

Even if a man was not let off by the jury, he could ask for help from the Church. Usually this meant that if he could

▲ Many small offences were punished by death. But for crimes like cheating customers at the markets, wrongdoers could be put in the stocks (above) or pillory (below).

▲ The stains on the pillory were made by rotten vegetables and eggs, hurled by passers-by. Some wrongdoers had their ears nailed to the wood.

◀ This man is being punished for begging without a licence. In England an Act of Parliament stated that such men must be 'tied to the end of a cart naked and beaten with whips throughout the town till their bodies be bloody'.

► At the front of this German picture, a criminal is being condemned to death. In the background are some of the horrific ways in which he could be punished. These include being burned alive and being left to rot on a wheel. Look at the picture on page 17 to see men tied to wheels on the tops of poles.

pass a reading test, he was just branded and handed over to the local bishop. Then he generally received a mild punishment and was released.

▼ Mary Queen of Scots calmly awaits her execution at Fotheringay Castle, Northamptonshire, England, in 1587. She was condemned to death for plotting to seize the English crown from her cousin, Queen Elizabeth I. Death by beheading was quick, as long as the axeman struck firmly and strongly first time. Criminals lower down the 'Chain' suffered the slower death of hanging.

Witchcraft

The 16th century was a time of great hardship and suffering. Many people believed that witches working for the devil caused illness, death and famine. More people were burned as witches in the 16th century than at any time before, but the disasters did not stop.

There was no *proof* that witches put curses on cattle, or killed people by magic spells. But governments and ordinary people blamed them all the same. The main problem was how to identify the witches. They could be men or children, but usually they were thought to be women. This was because women were believed to be more wicked than men. A woman who seemed different in any way was suspected at once. She might be young and beautiful, or old and ugly. She might be physically deformed, or even mentally ill.

Suspects were tortured until they admitted to crimes that they had never committed. Some of the tortures are

▼ The girl in the chair is being 'ducked' in a river. If she does not drown, she must be a witch, because the devil is helping her to float. The male 'witch' below is being filled up with water. Eventually he will admit that he is a witch, just to stop the torture. The deformed girl who is being stretched will do the same. In England convicted witches were punished by hanging. They were suspended by their necks until they slowly strangled to death.

In 1607 Frans Francken the Younger painted this picture of a witches 'Sabbath', or midnight meeting. It shows many of the things witches were supposed to do, such as casting spells, flying on broomsticks, and signing agreements with the devil. People believed meetings like this really took place!

shown opposite. Another, the leg screw, was used a lot in Scotland and Germany. It slowly squeezed the calf until the shin-bone was shattered. Tortured like this, women 'confessed' to all sorts of crimes. Then they were executed.

All over Europe, hundreds of thousands of innocent women were killed during the great 'witch-craze'. Today this seems incredible and quite barbaric. But when times are hard, people often pick on those who cannot defend themselves.

▼ In France, young girls and old women alike were burned as witches. The fact that wars, disease and famines still occurred made no difference.

Popular entertainment

During the working week, there was little time for leisure. But on Sundays, saints' days, and the great Church festivals of Christmas, Easter and Whitsuntide people relaxed and enjoyed themselves.

They danced, drank, sang and played games like draughts, dice, cards and chess. For those who wanted more bloodthirsty pleasures, there were bear-baiting, cock-fighting and, in the streets of southern Europe, bull-fighting. Whole villages played a violent form of football. The most popular entertainment of all was the public torture and execution of criminals.

▼ *In this Elizabethan theatre the players are performing Shakespeare's* A Midsummer Night's Dream. *Performances had to take place in daylight, because it was hard to light the theatre after dark. The flag was raised to announce a play that afternoon. The trumpeters in the little tower heralded the start with a fanfare. There was very little scenery on the stage, and boys played the parts of women.*

◄ Some common pastimes in Tudor England: (clockwise from top left) cock-fighting, football, bear-baiting, dancing around the maypole and playing cards in the tavern. All these remained popular for at least another two centuries.

▼ This is a detail of part of a painting from 1560. It is called Children's Games, and was painted by Pieter Bruegel. Some of the games shown are still played today. Notice how some of the players look much more like miniature grown-ups than children.

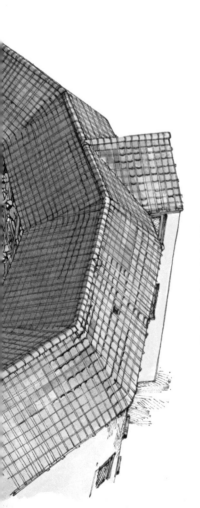

Most people could not read, but enjoyed listening to preachers and actors. Huge crowds gathered to watch religious 'mystery plays'. Less holy plays were put on by bands of travelling-players, in market squares and inn yards. Towards the end of the century proper theatres were built in the larger towns and cities of Europe. In these places, audiences watched plays by men like Shakespeare in England and Lope da Vega in Spain.

Entertainments for the nobles

Wealthy people enjoyed many of the same entertainments as the poor, like dancing and theatre-going. But nobles had more leisure-time than people lower down the Chain. In the Middle Ages, their main purpose in life had been to fight in their rulers' armies. Now most wars were fought by humbler, paid soldiers. New laws stopped the nobles feuding among themselves, so they had to find other ways to get rid of their energies. They turned to hunting – and to duelling. Duels were fought for the slightest reasons. Between 1585 and 1603, the kings of France pardoned 7,000 duellists who had killed their opponents!

But the nobles of Europe spent only part of their time killing animals or one another. They enjoyed gambling and games like indoor tennis. Many nobles were also patrons

▶ The virginal, or spinet, was a favourite instrument of Queen Elizabeth I.

▲ The viol was held upright between the knees and played with a bow.

▲ Lutes were sometimes provided in barbershops for waiting gentlemen to play.

▼ Gentlemen practising their marksmanship. They are shooting crossbow-bolts at small birds tied to the top of a pole. The man at the front is holding a longbow.

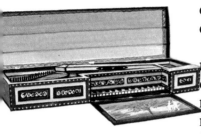

of the arts. They paid musicians, artists and craftsmen to come to their homes and produce works of art for them.

The greatest providers of entertainment were the rulers themselves. The nobles flocked to their rulers' courts, to take part in lavish pageants, masques and mock-battles. The rulers did this deliberately. While the nobles were busy enjoying themselves, they had no time to feud with one another, or to plot against their king.

▼ Woodwind instruments. Below: *a shawm, rather like an oboe.* Bottom: *a wooden recorder.*

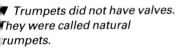

▼ Trumpets did not have valves. They were called natural trumpets.

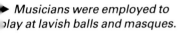

► Musicians were employed to play at lavish balls and masques.

► Outdoors, hunting was very popular. These men are hunting otters. Gentlemen – and gentlewomen – chased deer, hares, bustards, foxes and badgers as well.

▼ Rulers and their nobles enjoyed jousting tournaments. But some ended in tragedy. In 1559, King Henry II of France received a lance-wound in the eye. He was dead within a few days.

A soldier's life

The mightiest armies of the 16th century served King Philip II of Spain. Most of his soldiers were poor men from all over Europe. They hoped to make fortunes by capturing rich prisoners, or looting a town of its treasures after a siege. These soldiers did not pay taxes, tithes or rents. They were given food, shelter, clothing and hospital treatment.

But a solider's life was usually boring and miserable. His officers despised him, and could fine, flog or humiliate him as they chose. Wages were usually late, food and clothing in short supply, and diseases caused more deaths than enemy attacks. Most of the time was spent in starving one large town after another into surrender. There were few battles.

Soldiers were not allowed leave. They had to serve until the end of the war. Only those who were severely injured could go home early. Even those who survived could find

◄ *Spanish troops besieging the fortress of St Quentin in the Netherlands, 1557. The siege was followed by a face-to-face battle, won by the Spaniards.*

▼ *The soldiers of Philip II's forces in the Netherlands in 1588. There were also thousands of women, children, cooks, priests and surgeons.*

	Spanish Army
	63,455 Soldiers
	30,211 Netherlanders
	11,309 German
	9,668 Spaniards
Infantry	5,339 Italians
	1,722 British
	1,556 Burgundians
	3,650 Cavalry

Musketeer

Fighting with estocs

Landsknecht, using a two-handed sword

Crossbowman

◄ The landsknecht was a professional German footsoldier. Muskets were now replacing longbows. In the Netherlands, some musketeers had to pay for their own powder and shot. This must have made them think twice before firing!

little work when they got home, and often had to become beggars or bandits.

◄ Soldiers wore no special uniforms. This Spanish officer is wearing a bright red sash, to show which army he is in.

► Towns in the Netherlands were often heavily fortified. Philip II's armies could only take them by starving the townspeople. Even small towns could hold out for months.

Land travel

▲ Coaches had no springs, and were cold and uncomfortable.

Few people travelled far from their birthplace. In England, Cornishmen regarded anyone from the Midlands as a foreigner. There were, however, exceptions. Rulers regularly travelled around their lands, so their subjects could see them. Travelling players, beggars and pedlars earned their livings on the road; so did messengers, and the carriers of goods. But a journey, whether on foot, horseback or in a waggon, was slow and dangerous.

Wherever there were rivers or canals, bulky goods went by water. On the roads, pack-horses were used more than waggons because wheeled vehicles often stuck in the mud on the badly made roads. Any traveller might be attacked by bandits, and in wartime soldiers too. Travellers had to pay 'tolls', or fees, every time their route crossed a noble landowner's territory.

The nobles themselves had begun travelling in coaches. These had no springs or glass windows, and were very uncomfortable for long journeys.

Although people still travelled slowly, news was travelling faster. The map shows how quickly post-horses could get from one place to another. This was nothing beside the

▲ A merchant passes a peasant woman on her way to market. She was lucky to have the use of a horse. Poorer women made do with donkeys.

▼ French peasants were forced by law to keep local roads in good repair. But they could do little to stop them turning to mud in winter.

46

This map shows how quickly messengers riding relays of swift post-horses could carry news across Europe.

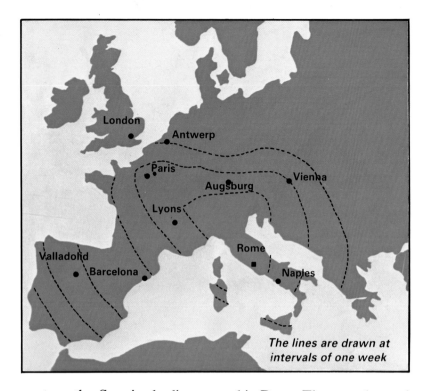

London
Antwerp
Paris
Vienna
Augsburg
Lyons
Valladolid
Barcelona
Rome
Naples

The lines are drawn at intervals of one week

Queen Elizabeth I being rowed down the Thames in the royal barge. She never went more than 60 kilometres from London during her reign.

The small picture shows a barge on the river Rhine in Germany in 1531.

system the Spaniards discovered in Peru. There, relays of men carried messages up to 240 kilometres a day – on foot!

Sailors and the sea

To meet the needs of trade and exploration, new kinds of ship were developed. The Spaniards and the Portuguese built huge sailing ships, called 'galleons', to cross the oceans. Many sailors died on these voyages. Some were killed by pirates or storms, others by disease, often caused by bad food. A survivor of Magellan's voyage around the world recalled that the hard ship's biscuits (their basic food) had become powdery, full of worms and contaminated by rats.

Another danger for the merchant fleets was 'privateers'. These were privately-owned English, French or Dutch ships, whose captains had been given royal permission to seize and plunder enemy vessels. The galleons used heavy cannon to fend off the smaller, faster privateers. But

▶ *Sailors on the cramped gun-deck of a galleon. One is mending a torn sail, made of leather. Another is eating dried biscuits and salted fish. Sailors often suffered badly from fevers and scurvy, caused by the lack of fresh vegetables or fruit. On long voyages, stored water went bad. It had to be strained through a cloth, to filter off the stinking scum.*

▼ *On early galleons the cannons could only be fired at very close quarters. So battles like this one still depended on the soldiers on board fighting hand-to-hand.*

English 'sea-dogs', like Sir Francis Drake, still raided Spanish ports and fleets with great success.

In the 1580s, war broke out between England and Spain. Queen Elizabeth I put the privateer captains in charge of the galleons of the Royal Navy. Their crews came from merchant ships. Yet this makeshift fleet shattered and scattered the great Spanish Armada of 1588.

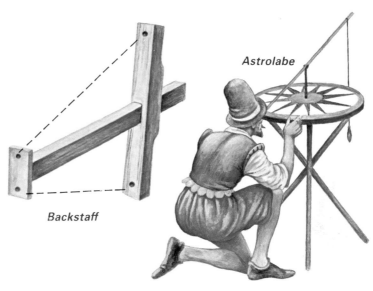

Astrolabe

Backstaff

▲ Ships sailing to America or the East Indies could not always keep land in sight. Navigators used simple instruments like these to work out where they were, using the sun or moon as a guide.

49

Merchants and traders

The new lands being discovered by European explorers meant great opportunities for trade. The profits from this world-wide trade could be enormous. The risks, too, were high. It only needed one ship to sink or be captured by pirates and a wealthy merchant faced ruin.

Many merchants clubbed together in trading companies, like the Merchant Adventurers of London. Sometimes these companies were granted royal 'monopolies'. These were charters allowing only one company to trade in certain goods, or with a certain region. For example, only the Merchant Adventurers could export English cloth to the Netherlands. The Muscovy Company was given a monopoly of trade with Russia, and the Eastland Company with ports in the Baltic. By the end of the period, a few companies based in London were handling almost all England's foreign trade.

▼ Cheaper goods from abroad could reach local markets like this one. But food travelled badly over long distances, unless it had been dried and salted. Most people still ate only locally-produced food.

50

◄ A rich woman visiting a London tailor. One apprentice is cutting lengths from a roll of silk imported from Italy. The master will then cut the silk into the shape of a dress. The other apprentices are stitching together pieces of a different garment.

▼ Shop-signs like these told people what went on inside shops. They were a great help to those who could not read.

► Coins were vital for trade. These coins were hammered out by hand. But after 1550 European coins were pressed by machines.

Groat (English)

Locksmith

Brushmaker

Sovereign (English)

Piece-of-eight (Spanish)

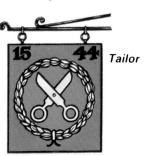

Tailor

Fishmonger

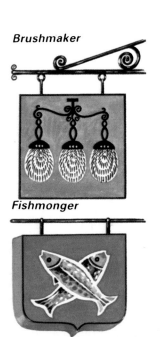

Thaler (Austrian)

Teston (French)

51

Great cities

By 1500, some of Europe's major cities had become very powerful. In Italy Venice and Genoa had huge trading empires and ruled themselves. In the Holy Roman Empire, 'Imperial Free Cities' like Strasburg were virtually outside the Emperor's control. But the rulers of Spain, France and England kept a much closer check on the great cities in their kingdoms.

In 1500, only Paris, Naples, Venice and Milan had more than 100,000 inhabitants. By 1600, there were at least eight more cities of this size: Rome, Palermo and Messina in Italy; London; Madrid, the capital of Spain; and the new trade centres of Lisbon in Portugal, Seville in Spain and Antwerp in the Netherlands.

Rulers began holding their courts in, or just outside, the great cities. The nobles spent part of each year in their magnificent new town houses, to be close to their rulers.

In contrast at least half the population of any city lived in real poverty. In times of famine, these people were the first to starve, since they did not grow their own food. Even when there was enough to eat, their drinking water was often poisoned by sewage. This caused epidemics, which raged through the damp, dark, overcrowded slums.

▼ This is a 16th-century view of Antwerp, on the river Scheldt in the Netherlands. Antwerp was one of the most important cities in Charles V's empire. It was full of warehouses, banks and industrial workshops. In 1576 the Spanish soldiers stationed in Antwerp went berserk. They raided and destroyed a large part of the city, and over 7,000 citizens and soldiers were killed.

But the cities also had attractions. There were taverns and plenty of entertainments. Above all, people dreamed of making their fortunes!

▼ The women at the front of this city-scene are wearing little wooden platforms under their shoes. These are to keep their feet clean and dry. Shopkeepers' wives pour their slops out of windows. An evil-smelling open sewer runs down the middle of the street. The closely packed houses are made mainly of wood.

Crafts and industries

The number of skilled craftsmen grew steadily throughout the 16th century. Each craft and trade had its own 'guild' to which the craftsmen belonged. The guilds had grown up during the Middle Ages. They laid down rules on standards of workmanship, fixed wages and decided on prices for finished goods. They also made sure that apprentices were given proper training by their masters, and looked after members who had fallen on hard times.

Each town and city had its own guilds. The members tried to keep craftsmen from other places out of their towns. But governments often encouraged people with technical skills to come from abroad. In this way, many industries spread across Europe. Glass-making was introduced into England by craftsmen from Venice. Germans started the Swiss clock-making industry in Geneva. Italians developed silk and printing industries in France.

▲ Many miners were peasants, sent from the fields when there was not much farmwork.

▲ Many people in northern Europe brewed beer. In England a licence was needed to sell it.

▲ Blacksmiths supplied endless local needs, from tools and weapons to horseshoes.

▲ Printers spent a lot of their time producing Bibles and prayer-books.

▲ Carpenters made furniture, and worked with masons and thatchers to construct houses.

▲ Shipwrights designed the galleons that took Europeans across the oceans.

▲ Cloth-weavers often worked outside the town, to escape the control of the guild.

▶ *This beautiful salt-cellar was made by a silversmith in Paris in 1527. The hull of the ship is the shell of a sea creature called the nautilus.*

▲ *In the first part of the century, Italian glassmakers were the best in Europe.*

▲ *Engineers built bridges and helped improve communications between towns.*

Most work of this kind depended on skill, not on complicated machinery. So it seemed sensible to have the best craftsmen.

▲ *Local blacksmiths sometimes also acted as vets, caring for sick animals.*

▲ *Minters made coins, usually by hand. Minting machines were common by 1550.*

▲ *A glovemaker. Elizabeth I liked wearing beautiful gloves, to show off her long fingers.*

New scientific discoveries

During the Middle Ages, most scientific knowledge came either from the Greeks or from the Church. Anyone who questioned this 'scientific knowledge' could be burnt as a heretic. But a number of 16th-century men *did* dare to challenge some of the age-old beliefs. By careful observation and experiment such men began to form their own scientific ideas.

In 1543, a Polish clergyman called Copernicus suggested that the earth went round the sun. Until then it was taught that the sun went round the earth. In the same year Vesalius, a doctor from the Netherlands, gave the clearest description yet of how the human body worked.

The Church and the universities did their utmost to stop this sort of 'heretical' knowledge from spreading. But they could not stop people being curious. Many intelligent young men, who might have become clergymen in earlier times, were now turning to science instead.

▲ This was one of the first accurate drawings of the moon. It was made by an Italian professor of mathematics, Galileo Galilei (1564–1642). Galileo used the recently-invented telescope to study the night sky. He observed that the moon did not have a smooth surface, but was covered with mountains and craters.

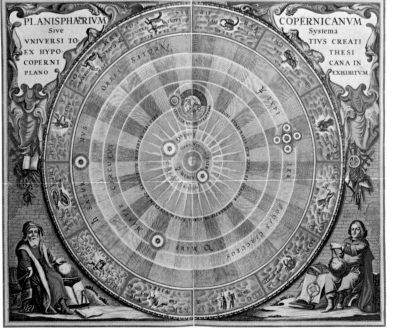

◀ Copernicus thought that the solar system looked like this, with the earth going around the sun, and the moon going around the earth. Uranus, Neptune and Pluto had not yet been discovered. Around the outside are the signs of the Zodiac. Copernicus' writings were not published until the year of his death. This may have been because he feared the Church would punish him for his 'heretical' ideas.

▶ This painting shows the laboratory of an Italian alchemist. Alchemists were scientific experimenters who had two main aims. The first was to discover how to make the 'Philosopher's Stone'. This would turn metals into gold. The second aim was to brew a drink called the 'Elixir of Life'. This would make people live forever. The alchemists failed in both quests. Gradually, real scientific discoveries and experiments replaced the alchemists' spells and mysteries.

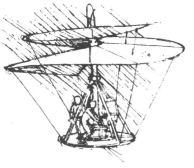

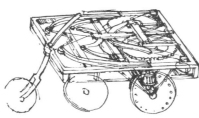

◀ Leonardo da Vinci (1452–1519) was an Italian genius. He designed a flying-machine like a helicopter (far left), and a sort of car (left). But he did not know how to power such machines. So they were not built until several centuries later.

◀ This is a drawing from one of Leonardo's notebooks. It shows his idea for an armoured tank. Tanks were not used until World War I, in the early 20th century! The writing below the drawing is very hard to read. This is because Leonardo wrote his notes in code. He wrote from right to left across the page, and turned each letter back to front.

Main events

1485 Henry Tudor defeated Richard III at the Battle of Bosworth. He then became Henry VII, the first of the Tudor monarchs.

1492 Christopher Columbus discovered America.

1494 Charles VIII of France invaded Italy. Start of Italian Wars.

1497–8 Vasco da Gama made the first sea voyage to India and back.

1509 Henry VII died. His son became King Henry VIII and married Catherine of Aragon.

1515 Francis I became King of France.

1516 Catherine of Aragon gave birth to Princess Mary, who later became Queen Mary I.

1519 Charles Habsburg was elected Holy Roman Emperor. He became Charles V.

Hernan Cortes and his men started to conquer the Aztec Empire in Mexico.

1520 Henry VIII and Francis I of France met at the Field of the Cloth of Gold.

1521 Martin Luther was outlawed in the Holy Roman Empire. He went on to set up his own Protestant Church.

1522 Ferdinand Magellan's ship, the *Victoria*, returned safely to Spain after the first-ever voyage right around the world.

1525 Charles V took Francis I prisoner at the Battle of Pavia in Italy.

1527 Charles V's troops ran riot in Rome.

1529 Turks under Suleiman the Magnificent besieged Charles V's city of Vienna, without success.

1531 Francisco Pizarro and his men started to conquer the Inca Empire in Peru.

1533 Without the Pope's permission, Henry VIII divorced Catherine of Aragon and married Anne Boleyn. Anne then gave birth to Princess Elizabeth, who later became Queen Elizabeth I.

1534 Henry VIII replaced the Pope as head of the English Church. England ceased to be a Roman Catholic country.

1536 Henry VIII started closing down the monasteries and seizing their wealth. He had Anne Boleyn executed and married Jane Seymour.

1537 Jane Seymour died soon after giving birth to Prince Edward, who later became Edward VI.

1538 Francis I and Charles V planned to invade England together. Nothing came of the idea.

1538–9 Bibles in English were placed in all English churches, by order of Henry VIII.

1540 Henry VIII married Anne of Cleves. He divorced her and married Catherine Howard.

1542 Henry VIII had Catherine Howard executed, and married Catherine Parr, his sixth wife.

1545 Members of the Catholic Church met at Trent in Italy. They suggested ways in which the Catholic Church could be improved.

1546 War broke out between Charles V and the Protestant Princes in the Empire.

1547 Francis I died. His son became King Henry II of France.

Henry VIII died. Edward VI was still a boy, so his uncle, the Duke of Somerset, ruled for him.

1549 The Earl of Warwick overthrew Somerset. Later he became the Duke of Northumberland and ruled England.

1553 Edward VI died. His half-sister Mary became Queen. She made England a Roman Catholic country again.

1554 Mary married Charles V's son, Philip of Spain.

1555 End of Charles V's war against the Protestant Princes. The Princes and their subjects were given the right to be Protestants.

1556 Charles V retired to a monastery in Spain. He shared out his lands between Philip II of Spain and Ferdinand, the new Holy Roman Emperor.

1558 The French seized the port of Calais from the English. Mary died and her half-sister Elizabeth became Queen.

1559 Elizabeth began to turn England into a Protestant country again.
The Italian Wars came to an end.
Henry II died. His three sons ruled France in turn until 1589.

1562 Catholics and Protestants began to fight one another in the French Wars of Religion.

1566 The Netherlanders rebelled against their Spanish rulers. The war went on into the 17th century.

1569 Elizabeth dealt harshly with rebels in the north of England, who wanted the Catholic Mary Queen of Scots on the throne.

1571 The Christian fleet of the Holy League destroyed the Turkish fleet at Lepanto, in the Mediterranean Sea.

1572 French Catholics massacred Protestants on St Bartholomew's Eve.

1580 Francis Drake became the first English sea-captain to sail around the world.
Philip II added Portugal to his empire.

1587 Elizabeth had Mary Queen of Scots executed.

1588 The English Navy defeated the Spanish Armada sent by Philip II.

1589 Henry Bourbon became King Henry IV of France.

1589 Henry IV ended the French Wars of Religion. French people were now not to be punished for being Protestants.

1603 Elizabeth died. The son of Mary Queen of Scots, King James VI of Scotland, became King James I of England. The line of Tudor monarchs ended, and the line of Stuarts began.

Famous people

Anne Boleyn married Henry VIII of England in 1533. She gave birth to the future Queen Elizabeth I in the same year. Henry had her executed in 1536.

Catherine of Aragon was the daughter of the King and Queen of Spain. She married Henry VIII of England in 1509 and gave birth to the future Queen Mary in 1516. She was divorced by Henry VIII in 1533.

Charles V became King of Spain in 1516, and Holy Roman Emperor in 1519. He was the most powerful monarch in Europe. He went into retirement in 1556.

Edward VI was the son of Henry VIII and his third wife, Jane Seymour. He became King of England in 1547, but died in 1553 at the age of 15.

Edward Seymour was a powerful noble under Henry VIII. He became Duke of Somerset in 1547, then ruled England in the name of the boy-king Edward VI until 1549.

Elizabeth I was Queen of England from 1558 to 1603, and never married. She was probably the best-loved Tudor monarch.

Ferdinald Magellan was a Portuguese sea-captain. He led the first expedition to sail right round the world, from 1519 to 1522.

Francis Drake was an English 'sea-dog' who led pirate raids on Spanish shipping. He was Vice-Admiral of the English fleet against the Spanish Armada. He became the first Englishman to sail right round the world, from 1577 to 1580.

Francisco Pizarro was a Spanish soldier. He led the tiny army which conquered the vast empire of the Incas in Peru, from 1531 to 1533.

Francis I was King of France from 1515 to 1547. He was a great rival of Charles V. Both wanted to be the most powerful monarch in Europe.

Henry VII was the first member of the Tudor family to rule England, having seized the Crown in battle in 1485. He ran the country efficiently, and died in 1509.

Henry VIII, the son of Henry VII, was King of England from 1509 to 1547. He married six times, and made himself Supreme Head of the English Church, instead of the Pope. He tried to set himself up as a rival to Charles V and Francis I, but had less wealth and power.

Hernan Cortes led a small Spanish expedition to Mexico in 1519. By 1521, he had conquered the entire Aztec Empire.

John Dudley, a Tudor nobleman, overthrew the Duke of Somerset in 1549, and took control of the government. He made himself Duke of Northumberland in 1551. He was executed by Queen Mary I in 1553, for trying to keep her off the throne.

Leonardo da Vinci was a brilliant Italian artist and inventor. He painted the *Mona Lisa*. He spent much time at the court of Francis I of France, and died in 1519.

Martin Luther was a German professor. He complained bitterly about the corrupt Catholic Church, then set up his own 'Protestant' type of Church. The Lutheran form of worship became popular throughout Germany and Scandinavia. He died in 1546.

Mary I was Queen of England from 1553 to 1558. She made the Pope head of the English Church again, and had subjects who would not worship in the Roman Catholic way burned to death. She married Philip II of Spain.

Mary Queen of Scots was Queen of Scotland from 1542. She was married to the King of France for a short time, and had a claim to the English throne. She was involved in several Catholic plots against Queen Elizabeth, who therefore had Mary executed in 1587.

Philip II, the son of Charles V, was King of Spain from 1556 to 1598. He was a Catholic, and waged many wars against Protestants and Moslem Turks. He sent the Armada against England in 1588.

Suleiman the Magnificent was Turkish Sultan from 1520 to 1566. His armies conquered huge areas of eastern Europe and caused panic throughout Europe.

Thomas More was an adviser and friend of King Henry VIII. He refused to accept Henry as Head of the Church, so was executed in 1535.

Thomas Cromwell was a very hard-working minister of Henry VIII. He organized the break with the Roman Catholic Church and increased the King's wealth. He was executed in 1540.

Walter Raleigh, scholar and adventurer, was a favourite of Queen Elizabeth I. He tried to start English settlements on the east coast of North America. He was executed in 1618.

William Shakespeare was an actor from Stratford-on-Avon and became the best-known playwright in the English language. He died in 1616, at the age of 52.

Glossary

apprentice A boy who was being trained in a craft or skill, for up to seven years.

cardinals Very important members of the Roman Catholic Church. When a Pope died, they met and elected a new one.

colony An area in one part of the world which was controlled by a ruler from another part.

feud A war fought between individuals for personal reasons.

Flemish Someone from Flanders. The area is now divided between the modern states of Belgium, the Netherlands and France.

Holy Roman Empire A collection of lands in the middle of Europe. The Holy Roman Emperor was chosen by seven Electors.

heretic Someone who disagrees with the teachings of the Church.

Jesuits Members of the Society of Jesus, started by St Ignatius Loyola. They were Catholics who worked hard to stop the Protestant faith from spreading.

masque A spectacular court entertainment. It included music, dancing and acting.

monopoly A charter which allowed a company or person the sole right to trade with a certain region or in certain goods.

post-horses Swift horses used by messengers to carry news from place to place. Teams of these horses were kept at inns along the main roads.

Protestants The people who complained about the Catholic Church, and set up their own churches.

seigneurial dues Payments or services that had to be given to landlords.

spices Pepper, cinnamon, cloves, etc., which came from the East and were used to season food.

tithes Taxes paid to the Church, either in money or in goods.

undergraduate A university student who has not yet taken a degree.

Index